ALLOCATION FORMULAS
IN
ACADEMIC LIBRARIES

CLIP Note # 22

Compiled by

Jane H. Tuten
Head of Technical Services
Gregg-Graniteville Library
University of South Carolina - Aiken
Aiken, South Carolina

Beverly Jones
Library Director
Al Harris Library
Southwestern Oklahoma State University
Weatherford, Oklahoma

College Library Information Packet Committee
College Libraries Section
Association of College and Research Libraries
A Division of the American Library Assocaiation

ASSOCIATION OF
COLLEGE
& RESEARCH
LIBRARIES
A DIVISION OF THE
AMERICAN LIBRARY ASSOCIATION

Published by the Association of College and Research Libraries
A Division of the American Library Association
50 East Huron Street
Chicago, IL 60611
1-800-545-2433

ISBN 0-8389-7812-6

Printed on recycled paper.

Printed in the United States of America.

TABLE OF CONTENTS

CLIP NOTES COMMITTEE

INTRODUCTION

OBJECTIVE

The function of this College Library Information Packet (*CLIP*) *Note* on allocation formulas is to identify elements used in allocation formulas and to provide guidelines for college and small university libraries that want to implement formulas in their budget allocation process. It does not attempt to evaluate either the fairness of the variables in the formulas or to evaluate the usefulness of the formulas. *CLIP Notes* "share information among smaller academic libraries as a means of facilitating decision making and improving performance. The basic premise...is that libraries throughout the nation are facing numerous challenges due to changing environments and that many of these libraries can benefit by knowing how similar institutions have resolved certain problems" (Morein 226).

Libraries have always had to determine how to allocate resources for the purpose of purchasing materials. As budgets shrink and as information becomes more accessible, objective methods of allocating funds become more alluring. Many libraries use specific formulas composed of quantifiable elements or variables for allocating part of the information resources budget, while others have adopted different apparatus. This *CLIP Note* reviews the nature of these specific numeric formulas and their use in college libraries today. Several questions arise regarding budget allocations: 1) Are allocation formulas frequently used? 2) What elements do other libraries include in their formulas? 3) How are elements weighted? 4) How often are the formulas and amounts updated? 5) How public is the formula? and 6) Are allocation formulas used for electronic resources?

BACKGROUND

Allocation formulas operate on the basic premise that needs for objectivity and equity may be met by the quantification of a variety of numerical data. The relationship between those data elements and the factors considered in the formula vary from institution to institution. The most common and desirable elements considered in allocation formulas have been the subject of numerous journal articles. Many libraries which have been the focus of the literature are located at colleges or universities with enrollments greater than libraries surveyed for *CLIP Notes* publications. *CLIP Note #22* examines the use of formulas in the smaller academic environment.

A survey of the literature confirms that formulas used for allocating the materials budget have certain core elements. Generally, those elements are number of faculty, number of students (often weighted by level such as graduate/undergraduate or baccalaureate/master's/doctoral), and number of courses. Numerous other variables such as circulation, cost of materials in specific fields, and faculty publication may be considered. The wide range of considered elements only underscores the individuality of each formula. How successful the particular formula is as a tool for the allocation process is certainly a local and subjective issue. According to David Schappert the "best formula is one that quantifies need with the minimum number of variables, since each variable adds to the time and expense of data collection as well as the number of calculations that must be made to implement the formula" (Schappert 141).

In an article published in 1989, John Budd and Kay Adams described allocation formulas in use across a broad spectrum of academic institutions. The article was based upon a survey mailed to over 800 academic libraries with minimum library materials expenditures of $100,000 a year. Budd and Adams identified the six most frequent variables found in their survey sample: number of students or credit hours, cost of materials, number of faculty, circulation by department or subject area, number of courses offered by a department, and number of students majoring in a department or subject area. They also note that the way "the elements are combined depends greatly on the type of institution which a library serves, the curriculum of the institution, the basic collection of the library, and the makeup of the student body, among other things"(Budd and Adams 387).

Specific case studies are widespread in recent literature. Examples are the University of Southern Mississippi in 1993, George Mason University in 1993, the University of Stellenbosch (South Africa) in 1995. These case studies enumerate variables used in the allocation formulas and personal experience with formula implementation in a historical context. A comparative study of allocation formulas using test data at the University College of Cape Breton (Nova Scotia, Canada) was presented in 1992.

Developing an allocation formula is a complex process which involves identifying which elements to consider and weighting them properly. Agreement must be reached before the formula can be a successful tool in the allocation of resources. Those involved in the acquisitions process must accept that the formula represents all parties and their interests fairly. In his article examining the aspect of fairness in materials allocation, Jasper Schad writes that "if there is enough money in the book budget to buy what faculty want, they are unlikely to be particularly concerned about how the budget is administered. When budgets decline and acquisitions drop, however, the same faculty members are likely to pay a great deal of attention to the issue of fairness and to scrutinize spending and allocating carefully in order to detect any sign of unfairness" (Schad 479). Schappert also writes that "formulas will not by themselves guarantee balanced collections, sufficient funding, or collegiality, but they will make the budget process less adversarial and arbitrary, and the acquisitions process more predictable and efficient" (Schappert 144).

As libraries face funding challenges, increasing materials costs across all formats, and the impact of changing formats with regard to methods of access and delivery, expenditures must be scrutinized. Many libraries implement an allocation formula to help in this process. In 1990, the Association of Research Libraries published *SPEC Kit #166, Materials Budgets in ARL Libraries*, to address a major issue for libraries -- that of "decreasing materials budgets and increasing prices" while "beginning to acquire and provide access to non-traditional formats and sources of information. They are facing decisions about how to fund these resources initially and on a continuing basis. At the heart of the matter are questions of retrenchment, allocation, and reallocation."

SURVEY PROCEDURE

In order to answer these questions, a *CLIP Note* survey was undertaken. The procedure used was the standard one for *CLIP Notes* Publications. The initial proposal and draft of the survey instrument submitted to the *CLIP Notes* Committee of ACRL's College Libraries Section was reviewed and approved. Surveys were mailed to participants in December 1994, and returned during December and January, 1995.

Surveys were sent to 273 college and small university libraries. The institutions generally ranged in size from 1000 FTE students to 5000 FTE students. This survey sample represented participants from the Carnegie Foundation for the Advancement of Teaching as "Comprehensive Universities and Colleges I" or "Liberal Arts Colleges I." These participants agreed to complete surveys for *CLIP Notes*. Requested figures and statistical information were based on Independent Postsecondary Education Data System (IPEDS) categories and definitions for the Fiscal Year 1993-94.

In addition to completing the survey questionnaire, some libraries using allocation formulas provided documents outlining their formulas or allocation procedures. Many of those documents are included following a discussion and summary of the survey results.

SURVEY RESULTS

The survey indicated 40% of responding libraries used some kind of allocation formula. A number of respondents to this survey had adopted a new allocation formula within the previous year. Others were in the process of developing new formulas. The advent of electronic resources will soon be affecting allocation formulas, their use, and their usefulness. The 192 surveys returned represent a 70% response rate.

General Information

Questions #1 through #9 of the survey attempted to answer the question: are allocation formulas still used? In general, allocation formulas are more likely to be used by those institutions with limited budgets. Seventy-six respondents (40%) indicated they had a specific numeric formula and 116 (60%) indicated they did not. Public institutions represented 25% (48) of the total response, while private institutions were 75% (144). Of those without numeric formulas, 22% (26) were public institutions and 78% (90) were private. Those institutions with numeric formulas included 29% (22) from public and 71% (53) from private sites. Public institutions are somewhat more likely to have formulas.

There is a positive correlation between having an allocation formula and size of materials budget in relation to the number of FTE students. The average library without a quantifiable formula has an information resources budget of $190 per FTE student. Those with a quantifiable formula have a materials budget of $139 per FTE student. The "no formula" schools have an average of 80 additional FTE students, 18 additional faculty FTE and an additional librarian. Schad's article cited earlier suggests greater attention to fairness results from tighter budgets. If fairness is equated with a numeric formula, this finding supports his statement.

Eleven percent of libraries with no quantifiable formula responded that they assign percentages by format, 17% process orders on a "first received" basis until money is expended, and 37% give priority to areas targeted for development. The remaining 35% indicated assorted approaches: "everything has priority over monographs," "historical performance and estimates of future needs," "response to accrediting agencies and new programs," "we annually target certain amounts to be spent in certain formats and in certain subject areas," and finally "the advent of electronic information services has resulted in a budget developed to meet the financial demands of electronic sources with a decreasing book budget." Responses of those libraries using quantifiable formulas are discussed in the remainder of this document.

Portion of Budget and Availability of Information

Questions #10 through #16 looked at how public the allocation formula is at an institution. Generally the formula is made public, to interested parties, in the spirit of openness and communication. Most libraries (51) allocate between 26% and 75% of the information resources budget using their formula. This means 69% of the respondents allocated the middle range using the formula.

The largest percentage of libraries reserve between 25% and 50% for expenditure by librarians. A majority do this outside the formula. Faculty expenditure of the library's materials budget divides almost equally between 26% - 50% and 51% - 75%. Sixty-five percent of the libraries fall in these categories.

Ninety-one percent of the libraries make the formula available to faculty. A far smaller majority (65%) makes the resulting budget figures available outside the department receiving the allocation. Actual numbers used in the formula are made available to the faculty by a minority of libraries (36%). In general, these decisions revolve around concern for potential divisiveness versus freedom of information.

When it comes to methods of expending the allocated resources, faculty suggest titles for purchase in 28% of the responding libraries; faculty and librarians negotiate in 25% of the libraries; and exclusive control of departmental allocation is held by faculty selectors in 15% of the libraries. In summary, the majority use some form of consensus for materials selection.

Elements and Use of the Formula

The survey examined the elements included in allocation formulas, how the elements are weighted, and if the formulas were used for electronic resources in questions #17 through #22 and in questions #28 and #29. Cost of books and numbers of faculty and students in the discipline are the more popular elements. Formulas that weight elements do so most often by course level. Very little use of formulas for electronic resources has been incorporated so far, although a number of respondents were concerned about this factor.

Elements included in formulas most often are average cost of books in a field, FTE faculty, circulation statistics, and student credit hours. If the data were available, one third of the respondents would add other elements, usually a usage factor. These "usage factors" included serials use, use of reference materials, circulation, or term paper bibliographies as an indication of usage.

Two-thirds of the libraries weight elements. Course level (upper, lower, graduate) is the most frequently used weighting factor in the sample formulas. Some formulas assigned weights to factors such as publications in field and number of faculty in the field. One library applied "discretionary factors" of 1, 3, or 4 as a weight. No explanation of the phrase "discretionary factors" was offered. Most respondents believe they now use an equitable formula.

Seventy-five respondents use the formula to purchase monographs. Fewer libraries include media, CD-ROMS, serials and periodical subscriptions, microform and government documents, in that order. Other factors affecting the formula include perceived equity, use, and outside factors such as accreditation or new faculty. A few libraries have a separate allocation formula for specific areas. These include reference, new programs, instructional media, periodicals, literature, and interdisciplinary studies. Only two, Cardinal Stritch College in Milwaukee, Wisconsin, and Northwestern College in Orange City, Iowa, have a separate formula for electronic resources. Neither submitted documents for inclusion in this *CLIP Note*. However, thirty-one of the respondents purchase materials in electronic format with money allocated by the formula.

Revision of the Formula

Questions #23 through 27 were designed to determine how often formulas and the variable elements were updated. In general, both the formulas and the numbers used for calculation in the formulas are revised frequently. Questions on frequency of revision of the formula indicate that 32% of the libraries revise annually. Another 24% revise more frequently than every five years. The numbers in the formula are usually revised annually by 80% of the respondents. Most formulas have been revised within the past year.

When the formula is to be revised, librarians make the revisions most frequently. The questionnaire did not differentiate between "librarians" and "library director." (All "library director" responses were added to the "librarians" category.) Sixty-nine libraries indicated librarians or the library director make revisions to the formula. Faculty participate in the revision process in 25 of the libraries and administration in 7 of the libraries. Eighteen libraries chose "other" to indicate that a faculty library committee does the revision.

Selection of Documents

A variety of documents representing many different types and methods of using formulas in the budget process were contributed by respondents. Weighted and unweighted mathematical formulas, formulas based on strict percentages, and descriptive types are all represented in the DOCUMENTS section of this *CLIP Note*. In some instances sample worksheets are included along with the allocation formula.

In a weighted formula the variables or elements are assigned coefficients or constants indicating weight. The coefficient is adjusted according to the importance of each variable, as perceived by those implementing the formula. An element is judged more, or perhaps less, important than other elements and given greater, or less, weight. The major advantage in using a weighted formula is that libraries implementing the formula can assign importance to variables deemed valuable to a particular institution. A disadvantage to the weighted formula is that in order for it to be a successful tool in the allocation of funds, all parties involved in the use of the formula must agree on the constants or weights assigned to the variables.

Unweighted formulas consist of variables judged to be of significant and equivalent importance. The advantage to the formula in which variables do not carry weights is that all items are assigned equality of value in the formula, bypassing potential arguments concerning value. Elements valued no more than others will result in a simplification of the quantification process.

Percentage-based formulas are characterized by variables assigned specific portions or percentages of the budget being allocated. Percentage-based formulas are straightforward and easily applied, needing little explanation. They are, however, quite similar to the weighted formula. Certain variables are considered more, or less, important than others and assigned greater or lesser portions of the budget in the allocation. The advantages and the disadvantages are the same as for weighted formulas. The advantage is the ability to assign a greater value with a higher percentage, while the disadvantage is clearly the need to reach agreement on which items are more important than others in the allocation of the budget. In another type of percentage-based formula, the discipline receives the same percentage of the library materials budget as it receives of the institutions' instructional budget (Schappert 1989).

The descriptive documents are narratives that describe the method by which funds are allocated in a library. These documents are unaccompanied by a specific mathematical formula, but allocate funds in a predetermined manner.

Conclusion

Allocation formulas are used by some libraries as a quantifiable method for the division of funds for expenditure. A somewhat larger percentage of public institutions use formulas. The formulas in use vary widely in their design, but are evidence of their continued popularity, specifically among schools with limited information resource budgets. Budd and Adams noted in their 1989 article that "the use of formulas appears to be most prevalent among those libraries which are neither too large to employ diversity in resource management nor too small for a formula to be feasible" (Budd and Adams 389).

The survey identified cost of books and number of faculty and students in the department as the most commonly used elements. Course level was the most popular weighting factor. Both formulas and amounts are updated frequently with newer formats for information being included. Generally, formulas are public information. With the increased need for fiscal accountability and the desire to be both expeditious and fair in the purchase of resources, allocation formulas are perceived by many as an equitable way to divide the ever smaller materials budget.

In conclusion, academic libraries with fewer resources resort to quantifiable methods in order to provide an allocation process perceived as fair. Most are still looking for an equitable means of dealing with the expenses associated with emerging technologies.

SELECTED BIBLIOGRAPHY

General

Budd, John. "Allocation formulas in the literature: A review ." *Library Acquisitions* 15 (1991): 95-107.

    A useful bibliographical essay that evaluates a number of formulas.

Budd, John M. and Kay Adams. "Allocation formulas in practice." *Library Acquisitions: Practice & Theory* 13 (1989): 381-390.

    Formulas using a variety of different weights and variables are presented. Libraries with budgets of $100,000 or more were surveyed.

Materials budgets in ARL libraries. ARL SPEC Kit 166. Washington: Association of Research Libraries, Office of Management Studies, 1990.

    This document addresses the topics of 1) acquisitions and materials budget funding, 2) sources of budget funds, and 3) the policies/procedures that guide the allocation and expenditure of the funds.

Morein, P. Grady. "What is a *CLIP Note?*" *College & Research Libraries News* 46 (1985): 226-229.

    Potential compilers need to look at Morein's article which provides an explanation of the purpose and history of the *CLIP Notes* series.

Schad, Jasper G. "Fairness in book fund allocation." *College and Research Libraries* 48 (1987): 479-486.

    A definitive discussion of fairness and equity issues as they relate to the allocation of budgets is presented in this thought-provoking article.

Schappert, David G. "Allocation formulas: The core of the acquisitions process." In *Operations handbook for the small academic library*, edited by Gerald B. McCabe, 137-44. New York: Greenwood Press, 1989.

    Formula types, the advantages and disadvantages associated with the use of formulas, and the reasons for implementing allocation formulas form the basis for this chapter.

Warner, Alice Sizer. "Library budget primer." *Wilson Library Bulletin* 67 (1993): 44-46.

> The advantages and disadvantages of six types of budgets used by different kinds of libraries are examined.

Werking, Richard Hume. "Allocating the academic library's book budget: Historical perspectives and current reflections." *Journal of Academic Librarianship* 14 (1988): 140-144.

> Werking's article presents a historical overview and current concerns in the allocation of budgets. Major issues such as faculty spending versus library spending and allocation by "head-count factors" are examined.

Case Studies

Allem, William R., Daniel L. Kniesner, and Virginia O'Herron. "Developing a quantitative formula for the book collection in small academic technical libraries." *Science & Technology Libraries* 2 (1981): 59-68.

> Librarians at the Institutes of Technology of the Bell and Howell Education Group work with faculty and administrators to develop an allocation formula based on book classification categories and curriculum.

Bentley, Stella and David Farrell. "Beyond retrenchment: The reallocation of a library materials budget." *Journal of Academic Librarianship* 10 (1985): 321-325.

> Indiana University looks at the distribution of funds between serials, monographs and binding, and equitable annual updates of quantitative data, supplemented by a narrative justification.

Brownson, Charles W. "Modeling library materials expenditure: Initial experiments at Arizona State University (to create a management tool linking policy and selection practice while avoiding allocation formulas)." *Library Resources & Technical Services* 35 (1991): 87-103.

> Arizona State University provided the site for this interesting experiment with the creation of a management tool that linked policy and selection practice. The purpose was to avoid the use of an allocation formula.

Cubberley, Carol. "Allocating the materials funds using total cost of materials." *Journal of Academic Librarianship* 19 (1993): 16-21.

> A formula-based plan using program data and price information for the redirection of resources at the University of Southern Mississippi.

Durckheim-Montmartin, Max E. Graf Eckbrecht von, J. Hennie Viljoen, Lezanne Human and Gerhard Geldenhuys. "Library materials fund allocation: A case study." *Journal of Academic Librarianship* 21 (1995): 39-42.

> The University of Stollenbosch, South Africa, creates and implements a formula. The article discusses the database and the allocation procedure. Positive evaluations of the allocation formula from both operational and management points of view are delineated.

Genaway, David C. "The Q formula: the flexible formula for library acquisitions in relation to the FTE driven formula." *Library Acquisitions: Theory & Practice* 10 (1986): 293-306.

> A committee of faculty and students at Youngstown State University allocated the budget using an FTE driven formula. This method is compared to a Q formula, which incorporates known variables plus productivity in disciplines and average title cost in each discipline .

Lowry, Charles B. "Reconciling pragmatism, equity, and need in the formula allocation of book and serial funds." *College and Research Libraries* 53 (1992): 121-138.

> A discussion of a matrix formula based on the needs of disciplines and publishing patterns used for resource allocation at the University of Texas at Arlington.

Mulliner, Kent. "The acquisitions allocation formula at Ohio University." *Library Acquisitions: Practice & Theory* 10 (1986): 315-327.

> A history of the development, use, and revision of the allocation formula at Ohio University. The formula is based on a division between supply (cost of materials) and demand (circulation, ILL, enrollment, faculty).

Packer, Donna. "Acquisitions allocations: equity, politics, and formulas." *Journal of Academic Librarianship* 14 (1988): 276-286.

> Western Washington University process, set in the context of economic theory and library literature. Extensive bibliographic notes.

Rein, L. O. "Formula-based subject allocation: A practical approach." *Collection Management* 17 (1993): 25-48.

> An allocation committee at George Mason University evaluates the suitability of a formula-driven allocation and examines a number of variables considered in the development of the formula.

Ward, Jeannette. "Rethinking the wisdom of collection development formulas." *At Your Service* (December 1993): 5-6.

Book and serials formulas at the University of Central Florida.

Young, I. R. "A quantitative comparison of acquisitions budget allocation formulas using a single institutional setting." *Library Acquisitions: Practice & Theory* 16 (1992): 229-242.

A comparison of seven allocation formulas applied to test data at the University College of Cape Breton (Nova Scotia, Canada).

Formula Data Source

McGrath, William E. "Relationships between hard/soft, pure/applied, and life/non-life disciplines and subject book use in a university library." *Information Processing Management* 14 (1978): 17-28.

Highly recommended by one of the respondents to the questionnaire, but not reviewed by the compilers.

CLIP NOTE SURVEY RESULTS

ASSOCIATION OF COLLEGE AND RESEARCH LIBRARIES
COLLEGE LIBRARIES SECTION/CLIP NOTE
QUESTIONNAIRE ON
ALLOCATION FORMULAS IN ACADEMIC LIBRARIES

Institution Name   *192* responses   *70% response rate*
                                 Public   *48*   *25% of respondents*
                                 Private   *144*   *75% of respondents*

Address
Name of Respondent
Title   Work Telephone
                                        E-mail Address
                                        Fax

1. Number of full-time equivalent (FTE) students

   average: 2501   *range: 522 - 7,764*   *185 responses*

2. Number of full-time equivalent (FTE) faculty

   average: 155   *range: 30 - 527*   *181 responses*

3. Number of full-time equivalent (FTE) librarians

   average: 7   *range: 01 - 24*   *191 responses*

4. Total library operating expenditures

   average: $987,887   *range: $83,300 - $3,354,625*   *189 responses*

5. Total book expenditures

   average: $155,380   *range: $15,325 - $1,172,890*   *187 responses*

6. Total serials subscriptions expenditures

   average: $163,950   *range: $7,700 - $776,360*   *188 responses*

7. Total computer files and search services expenditures

   average: $23,767   *range: $0 - $119,951*   *174 responses*

8. Total information resources (materials) budget

   average: $362,011   range: $6,200 - $1,547,899   *181 responses*

9. Is a specific numerical formula used to allocate your information resources budget?

   192 responses   40%   Yes   76
                        60%   No   116

   If you answered yes to #9, please continue with question #10.

   If you answered no to #9, how is your budget expended? Circle all that apply.

   144 responses

11%	Assigned percentages by format	16
17%	Orders processed on "first received" basis until money expended	24
37%	Priority given areas targeted for development	54
35%	Other. Please explain.	50

   -departments are assigned a percentage
   -selection by subject specialists and acquisition librarian
   -everything has priority over monographs
   -historical performance and estimates of future needs
   -response to accrediting agencies and new programs
   -we annually target certain amounts to be spent in certain formats and in certain
       subject areas
   -historic allocations maintained
   -the advent of electronic information services has resulted in a budget developed
       to meet the financial demands of electronic sources with a decreasing
       book budget.

Please stop here if you answered no to #9. Thank you and return these two pages.

10. What percentage of the information resources budget is allocated using the formula?

    74 responses

11%	Less than 25%	8
39%	26 - 50%	29
30%	51 - 75%	22
16%	76 - 100%	12
4%	No set amount	3

11. What percentage of the information resources budget is reserved for expenditure by
    librarians?

    73 responses

25%	Less than 25%	18
34%	26 - 50%	25
23%	51 - 75%	17
7%	76 - 100%	5
11%	No set amount	8

Is this outside the formula?	*75%*	Yes	55
	25%	No	18

12. If faculty are involved in the selection process, what portion of your library's
    material budget is reserved for faculty expenditure?

    73 responses

18%	Less than 25%	13
33%	26 - 50%	24
32%	51 - 75%	23
8%	76 - 100%	6
9%	No set amount	7

13. Do you explain or make the formula available to faculty?

    77 responses

91%	Yes	70
9%	No	7

    If yes, why?

    -the library committee helped to design the formula
    -accountability
    -was recently introduced and particularly where amounts went down from
    *   previous years, they needed to see the equity in it*
    -so they will understand that objective factors determine the allocation of the
    *   budget*
    -mainly for their input or insight
    -to share public information
    -to insure their understanding and support

If no, why not?

-it would cause problems
-no one has asked for it

14. Do you make the resulting budget figures available to faculty outside the department receiving the allocation?

75 responses

65%	Yes	49
35%	No	26

If yes, why?

-information, explanation
-prevents speculation
-many of our professional programs accreditation reviews require the
information

If no, why not?

-no one has asked for this data
-has always been considered confidential information
-it would cause problems
-don't think it is necessary. Library committee knows and has approved.

15. Do you make the actual numbers used in the formula available to the faculty in the relevant department only?

72 responses

36%	Yes	26
64%	No	46

If yes, why?

-common sense
-considered confidential
-to avoid questioning of the formula

If no, why not?

-I think secrecy in this area could cause a lot of problems.
-departments should know bases for allocations across the board

-want broader understanding and acceptance
-they need to see the big picture, not just their department .

16. How are the allocation figures expended? Circle all that apply.

76 responses

38%	Exclusive control of departmental allocation by faculty selectors	29
71%	Faculty suggest titles for purchase	54
63%	Negotiation (i.e. faculty and librarians work together)	48
12%	Librarians exclusively control	9
18%	Other (please explain)	14

-Director has veto power but is seldom used
-the approach is dictated by the desires and practices of individual departments
-librarians expend when faculty did not
-some trade-offs may occur, especially at the end of the year

17. Identify the elements included in the formula. Circle all that apply.

76 responses

54%	FTE faculty	41
41%	FTE students	31
43%	Undergraduate major or minor offered	33
24%	Master's field with no higher degree	18
4%	6th year specialist degree field	3
3%	Doctoral field	2
33%	Number of courses taught within a discipline/field	25
53%	Student credit hours	40
26%	Average cost of books	20
62%	Average cost of books in field	47
7%	Inflation	5
3%	Value of the dollar	2
26%	Number of books published in field	20
51%	Circulation statistics	39
9%	Cost of periodicals	7
21%	Cost of periodicals in field	16
5%	Format of material	4
43%	Other elements. Please describe and give source.	33

-graduates
-ratio of upper level credits in each discipline to total number of upper level
     credits offered in all disciplines/departments
-adjunct faculty, credit hour per faculty

-number of declared majors in discipline
-percentage for serials in each department
-number of books in the collection
-special needs such as a new program or excessively expensive books
-estimated library use level weighted subjectively
-bookish factor (national shelf list count)
-departmental spending pattern
-dependency on type of published material of field (e.g. science has dependency
on periodical literature

18. Are there any elements you would add if the data were available?

    68 responses

34%	Yes	23
66%	No	45

    If yes, what are they?

    -serials use statistics
    -use of reference materials and periodicals
    -number of active majors
    -some measure of strength of collection in the formula would be useful
    -circulation
    -library usage indicated by term paper bibliographies
    -timeliness, currency of information as critical to discipline
    -ILL in the subject area
    -media costs, but figures are so varied

19. Are the elements weighted?

    73 responses

64%	Yes	47
36%	No	26

    If yes, how?   *See examples of formulas in the documents section.*

20. Do you feel that the formula you use is equitable?

    75 responses

77%	Yes	58
23%	No	17

If yes, why?

*-the formula takes into account a variety of factors; the weights assigned to
each factor are discussed by division chairs annually
-currently each faculty member receives the same allocation
-it is flexible enough to take care of changes but stable enough to avoid fads
-it reflects university priorities as seen in courses offered and faculty hired."*

If no, why not?

*-subject to many variables, who is on leave in a given year, new courses,
catch up and balancing collection
-because we deal only with the book budget in this formula, we don't take
into account the fact that some fields rely more on journals
-I don't feel any formula is "equitable," only serve to give the illusion
of equity
-we're stuck in a Catch 22: faculty in some disciplines don't encourage library
use because the collection in that area is small/outdated. Circulation is
therefore low, and the discipline receives small allocations
-more elements such as cost of books in field need to be counted; I'd also like to
count periodicals and CD-ROMS in fields
-it does not factor how courses are taught: lecture, case method, etc., the
importance of print literature to the discipline vs. laboratory experience, etc.*

21. What types of materials are purchased with money allocated by the formula? Circle
all that apply.

76 responses

99%	Monograph	75
30%	Periodical subscriptions	23
34%	Serials	26
32%	Microfilm/fiche	24
41%	CD-ROM or other materials in electronic format (e.g. computer software)	31
66%	Media, such as film, video, sound recordings, etc.	50
9%	Computer files and search services	7
26%	Government documents	20
1%	Document delivery	1
3%	Other, please specify.	2

-musical scores, maps

22. Do any other factors affect the formula or final table used? Please describe.

-I generally decrease PE allocation because of low demand and number
of titles published. I generally add a little to English and Religion
because of heavy use in research
-anticipated accreditation visits or program reviews can affect the formula's
results, usually in the form of allotments prior to application of formula
-past performance of spending: divisions will have less money to spend the next
fiscal year if their faculty do not participate in the selection process
-new faculty
-no academic unit can gain or lose more than 20% in any single year.

23. How frequently is the formula revised?

78 responses

32%	Annually	25
24%	2-5 years	19
19%	> 5 years	15
8%	Never	6
17%	Other. Please explain.	13

-we revised in spring, 1993; I don't intend to do it again
-looked at frequently with intention to revise but final decision is always
formula works well as is

24. How often are the numbers revised that are used in the formula?

77 responses

80%	Annually	62
13%	2-5 years	10
1%	> 5 years	1
3%	Never	2
3%	Other. Please explain.	2

-not known

25. When was the last time the formula was revised?

average: 1991   *range: 1984 (or never) - 1994*   *mode: 1994*

26. Who does the revision? Check all that apply.

75 responses

92%	Librarians	69

33%	Faculty	25
9%	Administration	7
24%	Other. Please Explain.	18

-18 answered "library committee."

27. How often does the actual allocation change?

76 responses

92%	Annually	70
5%	2-5 years	4
0%	> 5 years	0
1%	Never	1
2%	Other. Please explain	2

-with budget increases/decreases

28. Do you have a separate allocation formula for any area?

76 responses

20%	Yes	15
80%	No	61

What area/ areas?
-architecture
-classics
- literature
-women's studies
-instructional media (3)
-music
-periodicals
-reference (2)
-new programs (4)
-interdisciplinary studies
-administrative

29. Do you have a separate allocation formula for electronic resources?

74 responses

3%	Yes	2
97%	No	72

ALLOCATION FORMULA DOCUMENTS

WEIGHTED FORMULAS

Fort Valley State College

A unit of the University System of Georgia

Learning Resources Center
1005 State College Drive
Fort Valley, Georgia 31030-3298
(912) 825-6342 or 825-6343

LIBRARY BUDGET ALLOCATIONS

FORMULA: CREDIT HOURS GENERATED PER SCHOOL
            WEIGHTS - UPPER LEVEL COURSES (1)
                    - LOWER LEVEL COURSES (.5)
                    - GRADUATE PROGRAMS   (2)
         BASE ALLOCATION TO ALL SCHOOLS
         NUMBER OF PROGRAMS/AREAS IN THE SCHOOLS
         FUNDS ALLOCATED FOR LIBRARY ACQUISITIONS

A. The budget for subscriptions to periodicals
   MUST be encumbered prior to the allocation
   process to the various schools because of
   fluctuation of prices.

B. Each time a new program is established from
   departments in the various Schools, an
   examination of the core library materials
   (a budget amount_ Must be considered through
   the LRC Planning/Advisory Committee, the
   Curriculum Committee, the department head and
   faculty responsible for developing the
   program.

C. New journals Must not be added unless other
   journals of equal prices can be eliminated in
   the discipline. Journals can be added provided
   the schools are responsible for subscriptions
   on a long term bases.

FY95 ALLOCATIONS

(Department Allocation Formula)

Total Books and Subscriptions Budget

1. Funds for general subscriptions are to be encumbered first

2. Based on the previous year's expenditures, funds will be allocated to a general fund under control of the library staff for:

   A. Standing orders not assigned to departments (eg, biblio-graphic tools)

   B. Reference and other inter-disciplinary materials

   C. Abstracting and indexing materials, including CD-ROMS

   D. Microfilm

3. Fifteen percent (15%) of the remainder is to be allocated to equity fund under the jurisdiction of the library staff. This fund will be used at the discretion of the Director of Libraries to supplement expanding programs, new graduate programs, or other special needs.

4. Funds remaining are to be apportioned by formula to the departments offering courses. The percentages each depart-ment receives is to be based on three factors:

   A. 60% based on credit hours generated, weighted as follows:
      Lower division - 1 unit
      Upper division - 1.5 units
      Graduate division - 2 units
      Internships, Practicums, and student teaching - 1/3 unit

   B. 15% to be given as a special allocation to those academic departments which use the library as their sole laboratory. This factor is based on the amount spent per student hour for equipment and supplies.

   C. 10% to be given as a special allocation to those academic departments whose average cost of library materials was above the median for the previous year.

LIBRARY COMMITTEE REPORT
March 9, 1993

The Library Committee presents a draft copy of the proposed new Library Allocation Formula which will be implemented for FY94.

The formula includes the major factors which relate to library use by faculty and students. It is objective, consistent and fair. The first column in Table A lists the rankings assigned to the criteria listed in the second column. For each of the 15 departments, up to seven terms in the formula are summed to give a weighting factor. Each term is a product of the ranking and the ratio (or fraction) the department has in a given criterion. The weighting factor is then applied to the $66,400 budgeted for undergraduate and graduate programs. The example under Table A uses the Business Dept. to show how the weighting factor is computed. Table B lists by department the final weighting factors, discretionary factors, allocation using new formula and the allocations presently awarded for FY 93. Attachments 1 - 3 list the criteria values by department.

Several points should be noted here.

1. The criteria are for the Fall 92 semester. THE FORMULA TO BE IMPLEMENTED WILL USE SPRING 93 FIGURES.

2. Data for undergraduate and graduate programs are integrated into the criteria.

3. Rankings were adjusted so as to narrow the range between departmental allocations which resulted when the new formula was initially applied and those computed by the old formula used to compute FY93 allocations. This adjustment applied to both excesses and deficits. Since this is a new formula, differences in allocations from the new formula and the old formula will appear.

> Dale Cressman
> Pat Gannon, Chair
> Gene Granroth
> Laurel Stanley, *ex officio*

TABLE A

RANKING   *CRITERIA by Department*

.20   Number of courses offered.
.20   Student credit hours.
.20   FTE Faculty.
.10   Majors.
.10   Concentrations and Degrees.
.10   % Subject area cost of books are over the   average cost of
                 books according to the Bowker Annual of Library and Book
                 Trade   Information.
.10   Discretionary amounts to be allocated by HeadLibrarian and
                 Faculty Library Committee using heavy library use, research
                 papers required, new curriculum changes, etc. as guides.

100 %

EXAMPLE   *Business Department*

# of courses offered

$$\frac{42}{555} = .0757 \times .20 =$$

.0151   +

Student credit hrs.

$$\frac{1061}{15909.5} = .0667 \times .20 =$$

.0133   +

FTE Faculty

$$\frac{4.92}{81.73} = .0602 \times .20 =$$

.0120   +

Majors

$$\frac{139.7}{1035.80} = .1349 \times .10 =$$

.0135   +

Concentrations & Degrees

$$\frac{5}{50} = .10 \times .10 =$$

.0100   +

Cost of books over average

—

Discretionary Factors

$$\frac{1}{17} = .0588 \times .10 =$$

.0059

TOTAL

.0698

TABLE B

Department	Weighting Factor	Discretionary Factors	New Allocation	FY93 Allocation
Art	.0198	1	$ 1708.25	$ 1757.25
Business	.0698	1	4636.49	4811.67
CAS	.0824		5473.13	6006.60
Education	.1518	3	10,081.29	10696.86
English	.0922	3	6123.85	6415.56
For.Lang.	.0138		918.09	1118.25
IDS	.0078		519.69	0
Math	.0829		5506.33	4262.13
Met	.0517	1	3434.65	3514.50
Music	.0141		938.01	1118.25
Philosophy	.0173	1	1150.49	1118.25
Pyschology	.0863		5732.09	3834.00
Recreation	.0610	3	4052.17	4600.80
Science	.1399		9291.13	6479.46
Social Science	.1029	4	6834.34	8166.42
Graduate	0		0	2500.00

Fall '92
Departments

	ART	BUS	CAS	EDU	ENG	FL	IDS	MAT	MET	MUS	PHI	PSY	REC	SCI	SSC	TOTAL
#Courses Offered	6	42	44	88	43	9	4	47	32	11	11	60	28	60	70	555
#Degrees Concen	1	5	4	12	3	3	1	3	1	1	1	2	3	4	6	50

Notes: Minors not counted
IDS is really IDS/NSS

Faculty (does not include faculty on sabbatical or other leave)

Dept.	ART	BUS	CAS	EDU	ENG	FL	IDS	MAT	MET	MUS	PHI	PSY	REC	SCI	SSC	TOTAL
FTE plus PTE	1.0	4.92	8.5	11.75	9.25	1.0	1.0	10.44	4.38	1.66	1.0	8.38	5.43	7.49	5.63	81.73

Majors (Upper Division plus Lower Division and Graduate School)

Dept.	ART	BUS	CAS	EDU	ENG	FL	IDS	MAT\ CSC	MET	MUS	PHI	PSY	REC	SCI	SSC	TOTAL
FTE	-	139.7	191.9	233.4	63.3	-	-	28.5	71.1	-	-	135.4	67	54.1	51.4	1035.8

Student Credit Hours by Department

Dept.	ART	BUS	CAS	EDU	ENG	FL	IDS	MAT\ CSC	MET	MUS	PHI	PSY	REC	SCI	SSC	TOTAL
	216	1061	1526	2154.5	1932	177	156	2005	566	219	240	2156	616	1301	1584	15909.5

Excess over Average Cost of Books
Costs taken from *Bowker Annual* - see attached sheet

	Average	Excess	Difference	Ratio
Art	$41.29	$55.62	$14.33	.105
Math	$41.29	$50.48	$ 9.19	.067
Met	$41.29	$51.79	$10.50	.077
Music	$41.29	$42.92	$ 1.63	.012
Science	$41.29			.704
Geology		$64.02	$22.73	.166
Biology		$68.97	$27.68	.203
Chemistry		$76.24	$34.95	.256
Physics		$52.04	$10.75	.079
Social Science	$41.29			.035
Economics		$44.32	$ 3.03	.022
History		$43.08	$ -1.79	.013
Total Difference			$136.59	1.00

Mabee Library
Washburn University
Topeka, KS

" Books and Research Materials Fund"

1. Scope of subject literature

   A. Average book cost for each department/school from the most recent complete fiscal year as a percent of overall book cost for all academic unit book purchases (locally derived).

   B. Number of titles published in each "subject" during the most recent complete fiscal year as a percent of all titles published for all "subjects" in which the library collects (Blackwell North America supplied data based on our "subject" profiles)

   C. A is weighted as 1, B is weighted as 1. A + B/2 = weight of 1 for this entire aspect of the formula

2. Credit hours

   A. Lower division credit hours by department/school as a percent of all lower division hours for the most recent complete academic year (locally derived).

   B. Upper division credit hours by department/school as a percent of all upper division hours for the most recent complete academic year (locally derived)

   C. Graduate credit hours by department/school as a percent of all graduate hours for the most recent complete academic year (locally derived)

   D. A is weighted as 1, B is weighted as 2, C is weighted as 3. A + B + C x 2 = weight of 2 for this entire aspect of the formula

3. FTE faculty

   A. FTE faculty by department/school as a percent of all FTE faculty for the most recent complete academic year (locally derived)

B. A is weighted as 1

4. Usage

   A. Class use for each department/school as a percent of total class use (locally derived during one library survey period each semester)

   B. Circulation by "subject" as a percent of total circulation (locally derived juring one library survey period each semester)

   C. A is weighted as 1, B is weighted as 1. A + B/2 x 1.5 = weight of 1.5 for this entire aspects of the formula

5. Factors 1 + 2 + 3 + 4 are normalized to equal 100% and applied to 75% of the "books and research materials" budget

6. No single year fluctuation of more or less than 20% than the previous allocation is allowed for any department/school

Methodist College

Davis Memorial Library
Proposal for Allocating the Monograph Budget
By Department

A study of existing methods indicates that the Colorado system could easily be adapted to our needs. It is relatively clear and simple, it is flexible, and it is objective. It is also as equitable as any allocation method could be, and accommodates a wide variety of relevant factors. The number of factors tends to moderate the extreme variations produced by relying on only a few factors.

The basic plan is to multiply the raw data percent for each relevant factor by an assigned weight for a factor point total, then add the point totals for each department. The department totals are then converted to percentages of the total points for all departments. The resulting percentage figure is then applied to the budget available for monographs and the consequent dollar figure becomes the department allocation for the fiscal year. All the required data is readily available from the Office of the Academic Dean and the Registrar or standard library sources.

As modified for our use, the plan would include the following factors and weights:

Factor (By Department)	Weight
1. Semester hour credits taught	1
2. Number of courses taught	1
3. Number of majors	1
4. Faculty FTE	6
5. Average cost of books (by classification-- per Bowker Annual or Publisher's Weekly)	10

Regardless of their content, all materials would be charged to the budget of the department requesting them.

DEPARTMENTAL MATERIAL ALLOCATIONS
DAVIS MEMORIAL LIBRARY

1) Using relatively objective data, to whatever extent is feasible within the limits noted below, and subject to modification where needed, the library will calculate allocations for monographs and non-print materials on the basis of a modified version of the Colorado Plan.

2) No department will be allocated less than three percent provided the need for the amount is justified.

3) No department will be allocated more than 9 percent of the allocations.

4) Departments must have 50% of the monograph allocation encumbered by December 1. Library staff will encumber sufficient funds for books in that discipline to bring any department up to 50%.

5) Any funds for which orders have not been submitted by March 1 of each year will revert to the library general account. These are normally encumbered by the library staff for materials in the same discipline.

6) Items of $100 or more or sets of $200 or more will be approved by the Library Committee.

Codification of modifications
made by the Library Committee
to original September 1980 document

April 1992

1993-1994 Colorado Plan figures
Departmental library material expenditures

Sources of information were:
-- faculty FTE - dean's office (number is multiplied by 6)
-- number of courses and semester hours credit - registrar's office
-- average cost of a book - Bowker's Annual
-- number of majors - spring 1992 from registrar's office
   (latest available)

	SEMESTER HRS	NO. OF COURSES	NO. OF MAJORS	FAC. FTE	AVG. COST OF BOOKS	TOT. PNTS	% OF TOT.	BOOK FUNDS	NON-BOOK FUNDS
ART	697	31	20	13.50	355	1116.50	3.00%	$765.00	$135.00
BUS,ECO,ACC	6481	146	357	57.00	434	7475.00	9.00%	$2,295.00	$405.00
EDUCATION	2007	81	139	33.00	407	2667.00	6.06%	$1,545.30	$272.70
ENGLISH	5271	125	56	57.00	398	5907.00	9.00%	$2,295.00	$405.00
FOREIGN LAN.	1668	70	28	28.50	377	2171.50	5.01%	$1,278.40	$225.60
HIST/POL SCI	5482	87	63	36.00	513	6181.00	9.00%	$2,295.00	$405.00
MATH/CS	3795	70	55	30.00	452	4402.00	8.60%	$2,193.00	$387.00
MUSIC	1466	88	20	21.00	481	2076.00	4.69%	$1,195.95	$211.05
PE	1609	69	64	18.00	396	2156.00	4.88%	$1,244.40	$219.60
HEALTH CARE	0	0	0	0.00	413	413.00	3.00%	$765.00	$135.00
PSYCHOLOGY	1765	30	32	13.50	410	2250.50	5.10%	$1,300.50	$229.50
REL.&PHIL.	3000	41	7	21.00	411	3480.00	7.93%	$2,022.15	$356.85
CHEMISTRY	839	17	16	15	625	1512	3.39%	$864.45	$152.55
SCIENCE	2980	45	66	18.00	537	3646.00	8.32%	$2,121.60	$374.40
SOCIOLOGY	3111	57	72	21.00	405	3666.00	8.36%	$2,131.80	$376.20
THEATRE&SPCH	1558	51	4	18.00	432	2063.00	4.66%	$1,188.30	$209.70
	41729	1008	999	400.50	7046	51182.50	100.0%	$25,500.85	$4,500.15

MSM Formula Number 23

Where: A = Interlibrary Loan Usage
        B = Cost Weight For Books (1/17)
        C = Cost Weight for Periodicals
        D1 = Student Credit Hours
        D = Student Credit Hour Percentage of Whole
        E = Faculty
        F = Formula (A+B+3C+5D+E)

************************Calculated Variables****************

DEPARTMENTS	A	B	C	D1	D	E	F	Portion Of Whole	Allocation
Business	0.138	0.05882	0.046	5503	0.10697	0.099	0.96868	0.08806	$15,570.60
Education Undergrad.	0.038	0.05882	0.04	1311	0.02548	0.028	0.37224	0.03384	$5,983.48
Education Grad.	0.01	0.05882	0.04	1044.4	0.0203	0.007	0.29733	0.02703	$4,779.34
English	0.065	0.05882	0.021	2275	0.04422	0.146	0.55394	0.05036	$8,904.05
Government	0.09	0.05882	0.037	1371	0.02665	0.028	0.42108	0.03828	$6,768.40
History	0.094	0.05882	0.02	3369	0.06549	0.153	0.69327	0.06302	$11,143.64
Languages	0.059	0.05882	0.021	2461	0.04784	0.071	0.49102	0.04464	$7,892.63
Mathematics	0.008	0.05882	0.136	1377	0.02677	0.035	0.64366	0.05851	$10,346.22
M.B.A.	0.049	0.05882	0.046	5462.8	0.10619	0.057	0.83377	0.0758	$13,402.09
Philosophy	0.046	0.05882	0.021	3042	0.05913	0.057	0.52048	0.04732	$8,366.32
Psychology	0.149	0.05882	0.089	1592	0.03095	0.028	0.65755	0.05978	$10,569.60
Rhetoric	0.022	0.05882	0.021	778	0.01512	0.035	0.25444	0.02313	$4,089.89
Science	0.069	0.05882	0.341	2899	0.05635	0.05	1.48259	0.13478	$23,831.23
Seminary	0.056	0.05882	0.021	12602.8	0.24498	0.092	1.49473	0.13588	$24,026.40
Sociology	0.08	0.05882	0.055	2304	0.04479	0.028	0.55576	0.05052	$8,933.28
Theology	0.025	0.05882	0.021	2259	0.04391	0.043	0.40938	0.03722	$6,580.45
V. & P. Arts	0.002	0.05882	0.024	1793	0.03485	0.043	0.35009	0.03183	$5,627.39
	=====	=====	=====	=====	=====	=====	=====	=====	=========
	1	1	1	51444	1	1	11	1	$176,815.00

PROPOSED LIBRARY ALLOCATION FORMULA–Revised
August 23, 1993

Allocation =

$$\frac{Books + Cost + Faculty + Students}{4}$$

where the

Books factor =

$$\frac{number\ of\ book\ reviews\ in\ related\ fields}{number\ of\ book\ reviews\ in\ all\ SAU\ subject\ areas}$$

Cost factor =

$$\frac{average\ book\ price\ in\ related\ fields}{sum\ of\ average\ prices\ in\ all\ four\ areas}$$

Faculty factor =

$$\frac{number\ of\ faculty\ in\ the\ school}{total\ number\ of\ faculty}$$

Students factor =

$$\frac{weighted\ number\ of\ credit\ hours\ in\ the\ school}{total\ weighted\ number\ of\ credit\ hours\ generated}$$

Weight:

Graduate credits x 1.5
Upper division credits x 1
Lower division credits x .5

ALLOCATION OF LIBRARY MATERIALS BUDGETS

Each fall the Associate Director for Technical Services prepares a materials budget request and justification for duPont-Ball Library and for Presser Library for the Director of the Library. Upon his/her approval, this is directed to the President for consideration for the next fiscal year (June-May). In the spring the Library is notified of the approved budgets: one for the main collection and a separate budget for the purchase of scores and recordings for Presser Library.

From the duPont-Ball Library materials budget, the Associate Director for Technical Services sets aside funds for general materials (including non-department specific reference), binding, and microfiche of periodicals. He/she allocates the remaining funds to academic departments for the purchase of library materials. The allocations are based on a formula which takes into account the number of faculty, contact hours, courses taught, number of majors, materials costs, graduate courses offered, collection need, and library research orientation of the field. This fund may be used for books, periodical subscriptions, or other library materials.

The school and departmental allocations include their current periodicals and other serials. Each department is notified of its allocation and the balance remaining for new materials. These allocations are an attempt to fairly distribute the funds to meet student and faculty needs as outlined in the collection development policy. Funds not used by March will be used at the discretion of the Associate Director for Technical Services to fill the outlined needs within the scope of the budget.

****

FORMULA FOR DEPARTMENTAL ALLOCATION OF LIBRARY MATERIALS FUNDS

FACTOR	WEIGHT
No. of f.t.e. faculty: % of total faculty:	4
No. of 100-200 level courses in catalog: % of total:	2
No. of 300-400 level courses in catalog: % of total:	3
No. of majors: % of total:	1
No. of contact hours: % of total:	1
Graduate degrees offered: 10 points for department:	1
Library research orientation of field (based on consultation with reference faculty and study of interlibrary loan statistics) maximum of 10 points:	1
Collection development need (new programs, new courses, etc.)maximum of 15 points:	1
Publication rate and cost in the field (subject's % of the total cost to buy all of the subject's U.S. book and periodical titles in that field):	4

UNWEIGHTED FORMULAS

Reese Library
Augusta College
Augusta, GA

The college allocation for library acquisitions is divided among the schools and departments according to the following formula:

$$X = (Y + A + B + C + D)$$

where   X is the allocation to department;

            Y is $1,000 to each department offering a major;

            A is based on the percentage of lower-division hours taught;

            B is based on the percentage of upper-division hours taught;

            C is based on the percentage of graduate hours taught;

and   D is based on special needs.

This formula was established by the library over 20 years ago. It has been adjusted regularly over the intervening years based on a yearly review, with modifications or reaffirmation by the Library Committee.

Once the allocation is received by departments, the method of expenditure is left largely to the deans as chairs, who deal with it as their needs dictate. The library does retain money for the maintenance of collections that affect the whole campus, such as the holdings in Reference and the Media Center. Policies defining the roles of librarians and faculty in the development of the collection are part of the procedures manual in the acquisitions department of the library.

AURORA UNIVERSITY LIBRARY

GUIDELINES FOR THE ALLOCATION OF MATERIALS BUDGET

• Approximately 45% of the materials budget is allocated to the Library for standing orders, reference materials, government documents, collection development librarians, and interdisciplinary materials.

• Approximately 55% is allocated to the Schools and Colleges as follows:

1. The current academic program units within the School of Nursing, the College of Liberal Arts and Sciences, the School of Business and Professional Studies, and the George Williams College of Aurora University are identified.

2. For each unit the following calculations are made.

   a. Percentage of FTE faculty members is obtained by adding the number of FTE faculty in each program unit and dividing by the total number of FTE faculty.*

   b. Percentage of course enrollments is obtained by adding up the total number of course enrollments in each unit and dividing by the total number of course enrollments.*

   c. Percentage of book costs is obtained by taking the average cost per book in each academic unit area and dividing this average cost by the total cost of all academic units. This requires some value judgments because our academic units do not always correspond to the book trade listing categories. For example, because there is no category for nursing, the category of health sciences is used.*

3. A "formula percentage" for each unit is obtained by adding up the three percentage factors listed above and dividing by 3 (an unweighted average).

4. This "formula percentage" is multiplied by the amount allocated to the Schools and Colleges to obtain the "formula based allocation" for each unit.

5. The "formula based allocation" for each unit is used as a guideline in determining the final allocation. Other factors taken into consideration are upcoming accreditation reviews, activity/lab courses vs bibliographic courses, and student use of the collections.

C. Deadlines:

1. 50% of unit allocations should be spent on or before October 15.
2. 75% of unit allocations should be spent on or before December 1.
3. 100% of unit allocations should be spent on or before February 1.
4. On February 2, all unencumbered funds are released to the general library fund to fill existing needs.
5. These deadlines are necessary to ensure that materials are received and paid for by June 30 (the end of the fiscal year).

D. Advantages of a Formula:

1. It provides a logical and objective distribution of funds.
2. It insures that all parts of a collection receive consideration and an appropriate share of funds.
3. It is relatively quick and easy.

E. Disadvantages of a Formula:

1. It may be difficult to collect necessary data.
2. It is difficult to assign weights to variables such as faculty, course enrollments, or book prices.
3. It does not allow a built-in recovery from years of budget freezes.

---

*Sources: (a) Full-time-Equivalent Faculty as generated by each Dean, upon Director's request in mid-September; FTE data is needed for the overall academic unit plus individual units within Civilizational Studies, English/Foreign Language, Psychology/Sociology, Sciences/ Mathematics, Business, and Communications/Art.

(b) Enrollment Analysis, fall of each year, Official Third Week Report; add IDS courses to English.

(c) "College Book Price Information..." Choice March of each year, or Bowker Annual.

SLC:11/22/93

AURORA UNIVERSITY LIBRARY
FORMULA FOR ALLOCATION OF MATERIALS BUDGET
FY93/94

Aurora University

PROGRAM UNIT	(1) FTE FACULTY		(2) CRS ENROLLMENT		(3) BOOK PRICE		(4) FORMULA % FACTOR
	#	% TOTAL	#	%TOTAL	$	%TOTAL	(1+2+3)/3
CIVIL. STUDIES	7.33	6.89%	365.50	8.40%	$42.24	7.07%	7.45%
ENGLISH/ FOR. LANG	5.00	4.70%	286.00	6.57%	$35.50	5.94%	5.74%
PSYCH./ SOC.	6.33	5.95%	503.00	11.56%	$40.40	6.76%	8.09%
SCIENCES/ MATH.	12.00	11.29%	507.50	11.66%	$56.70	9.49%	10.81%
BUSINESS	20.00	18.81%	781.33	17.96%	$43.40	7.26%	14.68%
COMM./ ART	6.00	5.64%	191.00	4.39%	$44.56	7.46%	5.83%
COMPUTER SCIENCE	4.00	3.76%	182.50	4.19%	$42.57	7.12%	5.03%
CRIMINAL JUSTICE	2.00	1.88%	143.00	3.29%	$42.07	7.04%	4.07%
NURSING	12.00	11.29%	248.00	5.70%	$41.29	6.91%	7.97%
SOCIAL WORK	17.67	16.62%	613.00	14.09%	$39.77	6.66%	12.45%
PHYSICAL EDUCATION	4.50	4.23%	162.50	3.73%	$39.55	6.62%	4.86%
TEACHER EDUCATION	5.00	4.70%	219.00	5.03%	$40.66	6.80%	5.51%
RECREAT. ADMIN.	3.50	3.29%	139.00	3.19%	$44.41	7.43%	4.64%
NEW COLLEGE	1.00	0.94%	10.00	0.23%	$44.41	7.45%	2.87%
TOTAL	106.33	100.00%	4351.33	100.00%	$597.53	100.02%	100.01%

evised 11/19/93

Aurora University

AURORA UNIVERSITY LIBRARY
MATERIALS BUDGET ALLOCATION BY PROGRAM
FY 93/94

PROGRAM UNIT	FY93 $	FY93 % TOTAL	FORMULA FY94 $	FORMULA FY94 %TOTAL	RECOMMEND FY 94 $	RECOMMEND FY 94 % TOTAL	DEANS' CONSENSUS $	DEANS' CONSENSUS %
CIVIL. STUDIES	$4,250	7.20%	$4,507	7.45%	$4,600	7.60%		
ENGLISH/ FOR.LANG.	$3,600	6.10%	$3,473	5.74%	$3,700	6.12%		
PSYCH./ SOC.	$5,050	8.56%	$4,894	8.09%	$5,200	8.60%		
SCIENCES/ MATH.	$7,000	11.86%	$6,540	10.81%	$6,600	10.91%		
BUSINESS	$7,000	11.86%	$8,881	14.68%	$8,500	14.05%		
COMM./ ART	$4,650	7.88%	$3,527	5.83%	$3,500	5.79%		
COMPUTER SCIENCE	$3,400	5.76%	$3,043	5.03%	$3,100	5.12%		
CRIMINAL JUSTICE	$2,600	4.41%	$2,462	4.07%	$2,800	4.63%		
NURSING	$5,750	9.75%	$4,822	7.97%	$5,300	8.76%		
SOCIAL WORK	$6,850	11.61%	$7,532	12.45%	$7,500	12.40%		
PHYSICAL EDUCATION	$1,550	2.63%	$2,940	4.86%	$2,300	3.80%		
TEACHER EDUCATION	$4,200	7.12%	$3,334	5.51%	$4,000	6.61%		
RECREAT. ADMIN.	$2,600	4.41%	$2,807	4.64%	$2,900	4.79%		
NEW COLLEGE	$500	0.85%	$1,736	2.87%	$500	0.83%		
TOTAL	$59,000	100.00%	$60,500	100.00%	$60,500	100.00%		

Revised 11/19/93

50 - Unweighted Formulas

Illinois Wesleyan University
Book Allocation Formula
October, 1994

The library faculty have worked all year on developing an equitable formula for distribution of the book budget among all departments and programs. The following is a draft of our collective ideas. We are looking for guidance from the library advisory committee faculty concerning the concept.

After reading many articles concerning book allocation formulas and talking with a number of libraries that use a formula, we have identified the factors we believe will best distribute the funds equtably.

Categories of data include:

Book $ -- The cost of books published in the past year in a given discipline (Art, Biology, etc.) based on data from Choice May 1994.

CoCrHr -- Course credit hours generated by each department or school in the past year.

Faculty -- Number of faculty employed in each department or school.

Majors -- Number of student majors in each department or school.

StudLow -- Number of student course units generated by under class students in each department or school.

StudUpp -- Number of student course units generated by upper class students in each department or school.

StudTotal -- Number of total student course units (both under and upper) generated by each department or school.

StuWei -- Student course units computed doubling the upper class students' number in the calculation. Rationale is that upper division classes should be using library materials more heavily.

Circ -- Number of books circulated in the LC classification scheme ranges associated with each department or school.

Using these criteria we looked at five published formulas. After analyzing them we agreed we wanted to make up our own. We took the best ideas from each of them and agreed on six criteria for IWU. In formula one we had three criteria: book costs, campus criteria combined (course credits, faculty, majors, and students), and circulation. In formula 2 we used the same six criteria but weighted the four campus criteria. We felt that two criteria that were campus statistics and two library statistics was a good balance. We wanted to give all departments an opportunity to use their strength toward the formula so we took the four campus criteria and divided by two. This calculation was then added to the book cost and the circulation cost dividing by four. Our recommendation is formula 2.

BOOK ALLOCATION FORMULA
RAW DATA AND PERCENTAGES OF CRITERIA

FY94-95

Discipline	Book $$	Book$%	CoCHr #	CoCHr%	Faculty #	Faculty %	Majors #	Majors %	StudLow #	StudUpp #	StudTotl #	StuTot%	StuWei%	Circ #	Circ %
Art	17937	7.84	39	5.41	6.57	3.49	67	3.34	249	309	558	3.50	3.65	2641	4.42
Biology	1207	6.21	35	4.85	4.74		205	12.02	442	398	840	5.27	5.22	1783	3.10
Bus/Econ	1996	8.72	73	10.12	15.14	9.78	380	22.29	793	1489	2282	14.31	15.89	3093	5.38
Chemistry	6491	2.84	20	2.77	5.43	3.40	47	2.76	378	210	588	3.69	3.36	879	1.53
CompSci	2792	1.22	16	2.22	2.43	1.52	27	1.58	207	130	337	2.11	1.97	606	1.05
Education	5331	2.33	24	3.33	3.29	2.06	54	3.17	77	235	312	1.96	2.30	2760	4.80
English	26209	11.45	71	9.85	13.78	8.63	95	5.57	759	683	1442	9.04	8.95	5273	9.17
For Lang	8459	3.70	60	8.32	16	10.02	38	2.23	825	447	1272	7.97	7.24	2723	4.74
History	41145	17.98	59	8.14	13	8.14	141	8.27	636	806				7025	12.22
Math	3639	1.59	32	4.44	7	4.38	64	3.75	779	824		4.98	4.89	1434	2.49
Music	7579	3.31	56	7.77	21.43	13.42	161	9.44	794			5.15	4.01	835	1.45
Nursing	6591	2.88	26	3.61	13		158		636	399				482	0.84
Phil	10058	4.39	26	3.61	7	4.51		8.27	1108	805		8.06	8.06	6953	12.09
P E	1149	0.50	6	0.83	8.14	5.10	100		303	267		3.76		1537	2.67
Physics	3198	1.40	21	2.91		3.13	48	2.82	119	100		0.75	0.82	2011	3.50
Pol Sci	23963	10.47	28	3.88	5	3.13	92	5.40	186	213	399	2.58	2.58	1600	2.61
Psych	6817	2.98	38	5.27		6.92	118	6.92	414	290	704	4.41	4.19	4638	8.07
Religion	5181	2.26	30	4.16	4.67	2.86	11	0.65	624	467	991	6.21	8.14	3564	6.20
Soc/Anth	15407	6.73	35	4.85	5	3.13	24	1.41	446	228	653	4.09	3.71	4315	7.50
Theatre/Ar	2741	1.20	46	6.38	8.43	6.28	67	3.93	284	309	274	3.50	4.49	3551	6.18
Totals	228681	100	721	100	169.64	100	1705	100	8168	7782	15950	100	100	57503	100

Formula:(((Book%) + ((Course Hr%) + (Faculty%) + (Majors%) + (Student Weighted%))/2 + (Circulation%))/4

1000*(D+((G+J+M+P)/2)+W)/4

Discipline	FY94-95	FY92/3	FY93/4
Art	$5,061	$1,000	$3,200
Biology	$5,692	$2,100	$4,000
Bus/Econ	$10,749		$18,000
Chemistry	$2,628	$1,500	$2,500
CompSci	$1,480	$500	$1,750
Education	$3,140	$8,500	$4,800
English	$8,500	$10,600	$8,300
For Lang	$9,281	$4,000	$4,100
History	$5,585	$2,500	$2,600
Math	$9,771	$4,000	$4,800
Nursing	$6,900		$16,000
Music	$2,824		$2,250
P E	$8,324	$500	$3,400
Phil	$3,081		$6,300
Physics	$1,192	$100	$400
Pol Sci	$2,403	$1,600	$2,600
Psych	$5,489	$3,000	$4,800
Religion	$4,002	$1,600	$3,000
Soc/Anth	$5,294	$5,000	$4,800
Theatre/Ar	$4,220	$2,700	$3,400
Total	$100,000	$65,100	$92,600

1994 bkforms

Lightener Library
Keuka College
Keuka Park, NY

Acquisitions formula for faculty funds:

$$Q + .15 \,(co/CO) + .10\,(f/F) + .25\,(s + sm/S + SM) + .10\,(ci/CI) + .10\,(i/I) + \\ .20\,(sch/SCH) + .10\,((bc + sc)/(BC + SC))$$

Q = Percent of Library book acquisitions budget
co = Number of courses taught per discipline
CO = Total number of courses taught
f = Number of FTE faculty per discipline
F = Total number of FTE faculty
s = Number of students served by each discipline
S = Total number of students
sm = Number of student majors per discipline
SM = Total number of student majors
ci = Number of books circulated within each discipline
CI = Total number of books circulated
i = Number of interlibrary loans per discipline
I = Total number of interlibrary loans
sch = Number of student credit hours generated per discipline
SCH = Total number of student credit hours
bc = Average book cost for each discipline
BC = Average book cost overall
sc = Average journal cost for each discipline
SC = Average journal cost overall

PROPOSED REVISION OF THE ALLOCATIONS FORMULA, APRIL, 1986

The proposed allocations formula takes into account the following factors: enrollment at the undergraduate level (lower and upper level courses), enrollment at the graduate level, number of undergraduate and graduate majors in a department, and circulation statistics by four broad categories (Humanities, Social Sciences, Business, and Sciences).

The allocations formula is as follows:

$$\frac{\text{Lower level undergraduate enrollment by dept.}}{\text{Total lower level undergraduate enrollment}} \quad \text{times 5}$$

$$\frac{\text{Upper level undergraduate enrollment by dept.}}{\text{Total upper level undergraduate enrollment}} \quad \text{times 10}$$

$$\frac{\text{Graduate enrollment by dept.}}{\text{Total graduate enrollment}} \quad \text{times 25}$$

$$\frac{\text{\# of undergraduate majors by dept.}}{\text{Total undergraduate majors}} \quad \text{times 15}$$

$$\frac{\text{\# of graduate majors by dept.}}{\text{Total graduate majors}} \quad \text{times 25}$$

$$\frac{\text{Circulation by area}}{\text{Total circulation}} \quad \text{times 20}$$

The values for these variables are added to obtain the total for each department. The departmental total is then multiplied by the average cost of books in each department (based on library records). The allocation is made by using the formula:

$$\frac{\text{departmental total}}{\text{grand total}} \quad \text{times (total funds available)} \quad + \$500$$

Unweighted Formulas - 55

Southwestern Oklahoma State University

ALLOCATIONS OF LIBRARY BUDGET TO UNIVERSITY/ COLLEGE
DEPARTMENTS/ DIVISIONS/ SCHOOLS IN A SMALL ACADEMIC
LIBRARY

Sheila Wilder Hoke, Library Director

The one I devised is based upon four components---i.e.
number of FTE faculty in a discipline, number of FTE
students enrolled in a discipline, cost of an average
book in a discipline, and cost of a serial in a
discipline. The FTE faculty and students for the fall
semester are obtained from the vice-president of
academic affairs. The book and serial costs are given
in the BOWKER ANNUAL. A percentage table is made for
each of these categories and a composite percentage
of the total is made so that a percentage can be
determined for each discipline. With the exception of
Health & P. E. whose table is swelled by enrollment of
students and whose 1% is given to Education that cuts
across many disciplines, the percentage table for
allocation is complete.

Percentage Table

ciences	Student Hours	FTE Faculty	Books	Periodicals	Total	%
iology	5.7	5.2	8.0	7.1	26.0	6.5
hemistry	5.6	5.8	11.0	14.5	36.9	9.2
omputer Science	3.7	3.1	5.0	7.1	18.9	4.7
hysics	2.4	2.8	8.1	14.5	27.8	7.0
ath	5.6	4.2	5.0	7.1	21.9	5.5
harmacy	6.3	9.9	11.0	14.5	41.7	10.4
ursing	1.1	4.0	7.0	8.3	20.4	5.1
llied Health	1.9	2.2	7.0	8.3	19.4	4.9
Totals	32.3	37.2	62.1	81.4	213.0	53.3

- -

umanties

	Student Hours	FTE Faculty	Books	Periodicals	Total	%
usiness	15.6	12.6	4.6	2.6	35.4	8.9
duc/Psy.	11.3	11.1	4.3	3.4	30.1	7.5
rt	3.6	3.3	5.3	1.6	13.8	3.4
.P.E.R.	6.2	5.2	2.9	1.3	15.6	3.9
ome Economics	2.3	2.3	4.0	2.3	10.9	2.7
ndustrial Arts	4.4	4.0	3.0	2.2	13.6	3.4
usic	3.6	8.1	5.3	1.6	18.6	4.7
anguage Arts	10.9	10.1	3.8	1.4	26.2	6.5
ocial Science	9.8	6.1	4.7	2.2	22.8	5.7
Totals	67.7	62.8	37.9	18.6	187.0	46.7
					46.75	
					400.0	100.0

Fixed costs----i.e. established serials, reference, standing orders, etc.----are subtracted from the overall library materials budget. Only a portion of money for currency is allocated. Thus allocations to the department/ division/ school do not reflect the actual money spent for a particular discipline/ division/ school.

Library Budget Allocations
1994-95

Total Books 1994-95 $ <u>41,000.</u>

          Library 40% $ <u>16,400.</u>
          Faculty 60% $ <u>24,600.</u>

10% of faculty's $ 24,600. is set aside for the Discretionary Fund, $ 2,460. leaving $ 22,140. to be divided among six divisions.

	1/5 Parity	1/5 Enrollment	1/5 Full-time Faculty	2/5 Circulation	Total
Business	$ 738.	$ 552.61	$ 483.98	$ 493.27	$ 2269.
Education	$ 738.	$ 627.44	$ 553.50	$ 751.87	$ 2672.
Fine Arts	$ 738.	$ 609.29	$ 622.57	$ 928.10	$ 2899.
Humanities	$ 738.	$ 668.18	$ 899.32	$ 2738.27	$ 5044.
Natural Science	$ 738.	$ 950.69	$ 1107.00	$ 857.26	$ 3654.
Social Sciences	$ 738.	$ 1018.44	$ 760.73	$ 3084.54	$ 5602.

Transylvania University

Library Budget Allocations, 1994-95

Course Enrollment		
Business	1038	12.48% = $ 552.61
Education	1178	14.17% = $ 627.44
Fine Arts	1144	13.76% = $ 609.29
Humanities	1255	15.09% = $ 668.18
Natural Science	1785	21.47% = $ 950.69
Social Sciences	1913	23.0% = $ 1018.44
Total	8313	

Number of Full-time Faculty		
Business	7	10.93% = $ 483.98
Education	8	12.5% = $ 553.50
Fine Arts	9	14.06% = $ 622.57
Humanities	13	20.31% = $ 899.32
Natural Science	16	25% = $ 1107.00
Social Sciences	11	17.18% = $ 760.73
Total	64	

Library Budget Allocations, 1994-95

Circulation per Division		
Business	624	5.57% = $ 493.27
Education	951	8.49% = $ 751.87
Fine Arts	1,173	10.48% = $ 928.10
Humanities	3,461	30.92% = $ 2738.27
Natural Science	1,084	9.68% = $ 857.26
Social Sciences	3,899	34.83% = $ 3084.54
Total	11,192	

Differences between 1993-94 and 1994-95

	1993-94	1994-95	Difference
Business	$ 2190.	$ 2269.	+ 73.
Education	$ 2597.	$ 2672.	+ 75.
Fine Arts	$ 2570.	$ 2899.	+ 329.
Humanities	$ 5363.	$ 5044.	- 319.
Natural Science	$ 3912.	$ 3654.	- 258.
Social Sciences	$ 5464.	$ 5602.	+ 138.

Emma Waters Summar Library
Union University
Jackson, TN

(Wellesley Formula)

$$X = \frac{A + B + 2C}{4}$$

Where   X = Percentage of the budget

A = Percent faculty of total faculty

B = Percent courses of the total courses

C = Percent student credit hours of the total student credit hours

The bulk of the book budget which is not allocated to departments goes for reference, continuous shipping costs, and targeted collection development areas (new courses or programs , weaknesses in collection)

Gregg-Graniteville Library
University of South Carolina - Aiken
Aiken, SC

ALLOCATION FORMULA FOR MATERIALS BUDGET

The library allocation formula at USCA is based upon a division of the budget between faculty (60%) and the Library (40%). Numbers used to calculate allocation amounts are based on the previous fiscal year's statistics. The formula takes five areas into consideration and all five carry equal weight. The five are library circulation, the number of unique courses generated within a discipline, student credit hours generated by a discipline, FTE faculty within a discipline, and a portion that is divided equally among all disciplines.

A= Total appropriation
B= Total number of disciplines
C= Total number of checkouts for all disciplines (one-fifth of the allocation)
D= Total number of unique courses (major semesters only) in all disciplines (one-fifth of the allocation)
E= Total FTE faculty in all disciplines (one-fifth of the allocation)
F= Total student credit hours (one-fifth of the allocation)
G= Equal share total (one-fifth of the allocation)
H= Number of unique courses per discipline
I= Number of checkouts per discipline
J= Number of FTE faculty per discipline
K= Number of student credit hours per discipline
X= Total appropriation per acronym

$$X=(G/B)(A/5) + (I/C)(A/5) + (J/E)(A/5) + (H/D)(A/5) + (K/F)(A/5)$$

Equal Share	Circulation Share	FTE Share	Courses Share	Stu. Credit Hours Share

PERCENTAGE-BASED FORMULAS

Arkansas Technical University

FORMULA FOR LIBRARY BOOK BUDGET ALLOCATION
(Revised 1991)

UNIVERSITY ALLOCATION

The university allocation for development of library book holdings is divided as follows:

If $100,000 or less, then:

General (Ref. & Stdg. orders)	=	25% ($15,000 minimum)
Academic Schools/Departments	=	75%

If greater than $100,000, then:

General (Ref. & Stdg. orders)	=	$25,000 + 10% of amount in excess of $100,000
Academic Schools/Departments	=	$75,000 + 90% of amount in excess of $100,000

ACADEMIC SCHOOLS/DEPARTMENTS

The amount allocated to the academic schools is divided as follows:

Accreditation Review	=	$1,000 to department needing

Remaining Funds:

Basic Allotment	=	15% divided equally among the academic departments (20)
Library Usage	=	55% according to formula described below
Relative Cost	=	20% according to relative cost by discipline as reported in the *BOWKER ANNUAL*
Majors	=	10% proportionate to distribution of majors by department

Library Usage Formula

STEP 1 > Assign a point value to each course which will be taught during the Fall, Spring, or Summer semesters of the next <u>fiscal</u> year to reflect degree of library usage[*]:

>   4 = graduate course
>   3 = heavy usage
>   2 = medium usage
>   1 = light usage
>   0 = no usage.

STEP 2 > Record enrollment for each course listed in STEP 1. Use number from last time course was offered or (if new course) a reasonable projection.

STEP 3 > Multiply enrollment (STEP 2) by point value (STEP 1) to determine total course library usage points.

STEP 4 > Add points for all courses in each department to determine total departmental library usage points.

STEP 5 > Divide each department's points by total points for all departments to determine an allocation percentage.

STEP 6 > Allocate the "library usage" portion of the book budget according to these percentages.

[*]   Factors to consider in assigning point values for library usage:

>   Term paper assignments
>   Reading assignments
>   Bibliographic searches required
>   Reference and informational searches required
>   Graduate level research required

Berry College

Memorial Library
Berry College
Mt. Berry, GA.

Allocation Formula for 1994-5

50%   Library and Media Center

50%   Academic Schools

    20%   Divided equally among schools

    20%   Allocated according to number of majors

    10%   Allocated according to FTE faculty in schools

    30%   Allocated according to academic areas in schools

    *20%   Allocated according to schools at the discretion of the library director

* Consideration given to previous year's expenditures, average cost of books, use of library collection, and graduate programs offered.

Larry A. Jackson Library
Lander College
Greenwood, S.C.

Factors considered in dividing book budget among subject areas, 1993-4

Several factors are considered in dividing the book budget among subject areas. The emphasis is given for each.

1. The subject in the curriculum at Lander--45.75%

2. The cost of books in the subject areas--6%

3. Use by students--36%

4. Emphasis at Lander--22.5%

These are the totals before deductions (total of 8.75%) are made for various reasons. The largest percent that any subject area can get is 8 percent. Subjects which do not offer a major can get no more than 1 percent.

<u>Subject offered at Lander</u>

2%	Major
4.75%	Graduate Program
1%	Minor/Other

1%   Average <u>cost of book</u> in subject area compared to average cost of all books

<u>Use</u> as determined by student circulation figures (if 2 subjects share the same circulation number, adjustments are made) :

.5%	over 2% of circulation
1.75%	over 3% of circulation
2%	over 5% of circulation
1.5%	over 10% of circulation

<u>Emphasis at Lander</u>

.5%	Number of graduates
1%	9 or more graduates
2%	20 or more graduates
2.25%	40 or more graduates

Courses offered, latest fall semester
Lower division

.25%	10 or more

Upper division

.5%	10 or more

Number of full-time faculty members

.5%	5-6
1%	7 or over

Factors considered in allocating the book budget to subject areas, 1993-4

The book budget is divided among subject areas by considering factors such as use of the collection, the emphasis given the subject at Lander, the average cost of books, and whether the book budget was spent in a subject area in the current year.

1. Majors are taken form the Lander College Catalog

2. One price indexes are used: U.S. College Books. This is from the latest edition of the "The Bowker Annual of Library/&Book Trade Information." If only a few books are published, this can result in a reduction in the total amount allocated.

3. The student circulation figures as given in the most recent annual report of the Jackson Library are used.

4. The number of graduates in a subject area is taken form the section on "Five Year Comparison by Degrees Awarded" from the latest edition of the "Lander College Planning Update."

5. The number of lower division and upper division courses is taken form the "Schedule of Classes" for the most recent fall semester.

6. The number of full-time faculty members is considered.

SOURCES CONSULTED

Annual Report of the Jackson Library. Latest edition.

The Bowker Annual: Library & Book Trade Almanac. Bowker. Latest edition.

Number of Graduates from Lander College Planning Update. Latest edition.

Lander College Catalog. Latest edition.

List of full-time faculty

Schedule of Classes. Latest fall semester edition.

Olivet Nazarene University

Benner Library & Research Center
Olivet Nazarene University
Kankakee, IL

Benner Library
(Budget Allocation Formula)

Steps in figuring budget allocations for departments:

1.   From total amount budgeted for library materials, subtract estimated amounts needed the next year for ongoing commitments to Periodicals, Serials, and Reference (CD-ROM subscriptions, etc.).

2.   Take 18% from the remaining amount to be divided among nondepartment areas (Curriculum Center, AV, etc.).

3.   The remaining amount is to be divided among the academic departments using the following formula:

   15%   Flat allocation (divided among departments)

   20%   Average book cost (using statistics form March inhouse budget report of most recent year)

   25%   Student credit hours (upper division (2x) and graduate hours (4x) given increased weight)

   25%   *Library circulation (from annual circulation report arranged by Dewey subject areas)

   15%   Graduating majors (using the average of the last two years)

* There are no circulation stats for the "graduate" or "adult studies" budget areas. These statistics are included in the academic subject areas (e.g., nursing degree completion resources are in the nursing subject area).

SUBJECT ALLOCATION 1994-95: FACTORS DISPLAYED   ALLOC95

TO ALLOCATE: $144,403.33*

EQU=Equalization; CIR=Circulation; ENR=Enrollment**; FAC=Faculty; PSB-Periodical & SO Burden

DEPARTMENT	EQU at 10.00% $14,440.33	CIR %	CIR at 30.00% $43,321.00	ENR %	ENR at 30.00% $43,321.00	EAC %	FAC at 20.00% $28,880.67	PSB %	PSB at 10.00% $14,440.00	100.00% DOLLARS	PERCENTAC
Accounting	$687.63	0.26%	$114.31	3.65%	$1,581.50	4.22%	$1,218.59	2.05%	$295.92	$3,897.96	2.70%
Art	$687.63	6.33%	$2,742.08	5.42%	$2,348.54	4.22%	$1,218.59	3.30%	$476.19	$7,473.04	5.18%
Business Admin	$687.63	1.21%	$523.35	7.55%	$3,269.86	4.22%	$1,218.59	5.35%	$772.11	$6,471.54	4.48%
Biology (& Anthro)	$687.63	3.56%	$1,542.51	6.37%	$2,760.14	6.75%	$1,949.75	11.02%	$1,590.73	$8,530.76	5.91%
Communications	$687.63	2.51%	$1,085.26	4.20%	$1,819.74	3.38%	$974.87	2.00%	$289.14	$4,856.65	3.36%
Comp Prog & Info	$687.63	0.54%	$235.78	2.94%	$1,272.40	3.38%	$974.87	1.93%	$278.15	$3,448.84	2.39%
Economics	$687.63	1.21%	$523.35	3.70%	$1,604.95	4.22%	$1,218.59	1.98%	$286.23	$4,320.75	2.99%
Education	$687.63	7.25%	$3,141.48	6.58%	$2,851.72	7.59%	$2,193.47	7.48%	$1,080.30	$9,954.61	6.89%
English	$687.63	20.04%	$8,682.10	12.21%	$5,291.31	7.59%	$2,193.47	7.30%	$1,053.81	$17,908.33	12.40%
History	$687.63	17.90%	$7,752.47	7.06%	$3,056.71	5.91%	$1,706.03	2.20%	$317.24	$13,520.08	9.36%
Home Economics	$687.63	0.89%	$387.00	2.09%	$907.14	2.53%	$731.16	2.31%	$333.40	$3,046.33	2.11%
Library Science	$687.63	2.62%	$1,136.22	0.19%	$82.32	4.22%	$1,218.59	2.11%	$304.97	$3,429.73	2.38%
Math & Engineering	$687.63	5.42%	$2,347.91	7.20%	$2,117.21	6.75%	$1,949.75	2.59%	$374.42	$8,476.94	5.87%
Music & Theater	$687.63	4.51%	$1,954.30	3.98%	$1,723.25	5.91%	$1,706.03	5.66%	$817.98	$6,889.19	4.77%
Nursing	$687.63	5.81%	$2,514.84	3.51%	$1,519.36	6.75%	$1,949.75	5.23%	$754.98	$7,426.56	5.14%
Philo, Rel, Classics	$687.63	3.33%	$1,443.34	0.32%	$140.65	0.00%	$0.00	0.70%	$100.47	$2,372.10	1.64%
PER	$687.63	2.73%	$1,184.42	6.29%	$2,724.16	8.44%	$2,437.19	7.12%	$1,028.29	$8,061.69	5.58%
Physical Science	$687.63	2.78%	$1,205.08	4.53%	$1,963.66	4.22%	$1,218.59	11.83%	$1,708.33	$6,783.30	4.70%
Political Science	$687.63	2.86%	$1,238.14	3.96%	$1,713.43	2.95%	$853.02	2.89%	$417.39	$4,909.61	3.40%
Psych & Geography	$687.63	3.20%	$1,384.12	3.85%	$1,669.27	2.53%	$731.16	10.81%	$1,560.37	$6,032.56	4.18%
Soc Work, Sociology	$687.63	5.04%	$2,182.92	4.39%	$1,903.69	4.22%	$1,218.59	4.15%	$599.92	$6,592.76	4.57%
TOTAL	$14,440.23	100.00%	$43,321.00	100.00%	$43,321.00	100.00%	$28,880.67	100.00%	$14,440.33	$144,403.33	100.00%

* Represents 2/3 of available funds. One-third is left unallocated.

LAVERY LIBRARY
ALLOCATION FORMULA FOR UNDERGRADUATE BOOKS

I.   DIVISION OF BOOK BUDGET:

     A.   50% for Library General (standing orders, reference, library science, interdepartmental, etc.)

     B.   50% for Departments

II.   FORMULA USED FOR DEPARTMENTS:

     A.   Basic allocation, 60% equal allocation to each department. PLUS

     B.   Size allocation, 40% based on formula average %.

III.   FORMULA AVERAGE % (recalculated every 2 years):

     A.   Number of FTE faculty (% of total)

     B.   Number of course offering sections (% of total)

     C.   Number of credit hours taken in division/department (% of total)

     D.   Number of majors in division/department (% of total)

     E.   Number of students enrolled in division/department (% of total)

     F. $\dfrac{A\% + B\% + C\% + D\% + E\%}{5}$ = Formula Average %

IV.   DISCRETIONARY FACTORS:

     A.   New instructors

     B.   New courses

     C.   New concepts

     D.   Nature of courses

     E.   College objectives

     F.   Departmental objectives

Todd Wehr Library
St. Norbert College
DePere, WI

Allocation Formula

Monographs Budget
1993-1994

Discipline:

Choice Book Categories Applied:

Number of faculty as percentage of total   x 20% =

Number of upper division registrations
  as percentage of total   x 10% =

Number of lower division registrations
  as percentage of total   x 20% =

Number of majors as percentage of total   x 25% =

Average cost per volume as percentage
  of total   x 25% =

NARRATIVE DESCRIPTIONS

Departmental Allocation Formula

The following information is obtained for each field in which a major is offered:

availability, the number of books reviewed in CHOICE in the field during the past year

cost, the average cost of books published in the field during the past year, as published in the BOWKER ANNUAL, "U.S. College Books : Average Prices and Price Indexes."

enrollment, the number of enrollments in the field during the past year (<u>not</u> fte)

use, estimated use of the library by students enrolled in all courses in this field, based on the syllabi, using the following weights:

> 0=no library use mentioned
>
> 1=reserve reading, either optional or required
>
> 2=outside reading of the student's choice, either recommended or required
>
> 3=short assignments requiring library resources, papers less than 8 pages in length or speeches of less than 15 minutes duration
>
> 4=long assignments requiring library resources, papers 8 pages or longer or speeches of 15 minutes duration or longer

For each field, each of the elements are calculated as a percentage of the sum. Those percentages are added together and divided by 4 so that when all of the field percentages are added up, they equal 100%. The total field percentage represents the percentage of the allocatable budget that can be spent for materials in the field.

((availability in field/sum of availability)+(cost in field/sum of cost)+(enrollment in field/sum of enrollment)+(use in field/sum of use))/4=% of allocatable budget

LOUIS L. MANDERINO LIBRARY
CALIFORNIA UNIVERSITY OF PENNSYLVANIA
250 UNIVERSITY AVENUE
CALIFORNIA, PENNSYLVANIA 15419-1394

412-938-5772   FAX 412-938-5901

Sept 27, 1993

TO: William L. Beck
           Dean of Library Services

FROM: Kathy Jokl
           Library Systems Analyst

SUB: How the Departmental Allocation Spreadsheeet works

     The departmental allocation spreadsheet requires the
user to input the following information:

1. A list of department names.
2. A code for each dept (L,S or E) indicating which type of
    books are generally purchased for that dept. (liberal
    arts, science, or education)
3. The number of students enrolled in each dept.
4. The number of majors in each dept.
5. A 'Y' or 'N' indicating whether each dept has a graduate
    program.
6. The total available dollar amount.
7. The adjusted amount (if desired) - This is a base amount
    given to each department.
8. The current average cost of a book in each of the three
    fields. (liberal arts, science, and education)
9. Four weights must be entered. Each weight is associated
    with the value placed on each of the four criteria. (The
    criteria are as follows: book cost, number of enrollees,
    number of majors, and the existence of a graduate
    program) The four numbers added together must sum to 100.

     Once this information is entered into the spreadsheet,
all of the calculations are performed automatically. The
results can be printed and changes can be made quickly and
easily.

The final amount designated for any given department is calculated as:

The (cost of a book in that department divided by the total cost of a book in all departments times the weight of the cost of a book times the total available dollar amount divided by 100).

To this amount you then add:

(the number of students in that department divided by the total number of students in all departments times the weight of the number of students times the total available dollar amount divided by 100).

To this amount you then add:

(the number of majors in that department divided by the total number of majors in all departments times the weight of the number of majors times the total available dollar amount divided by 100).

To this amount you then add:

Zero if there is no graduate program or (One divided by the total number of departments with graduate programs times the weight of the graduate program times the total available dollar amount divided by 100).

The adjusted finals column simply takes the amounts calculated above and adds the designated base amount for each department.

(FY 93/94) DEPARTMENT		BOOK COST	NUMBER ENROLLED	NUMBER MAJORS	GRAD PGM	FINAL AMOUNT	ADJUSTED FINALS
ART	L	$45	445	53	-	$353.45	$853.45
BIOLOGY	S	$62	2260	811	Y	$1,312.25	$1,812.25
BUS AND ECON	S	$62	1961	987	Y	$1,353.70	$1,853.70
COMM STUDIES	L	$45	1006	190	Y	$646.31	$1,146.31
COUNSELOR ED	E	$40	178	98	Y	$415.17	$915.17
EARTH SCI	S	$62	1390	144	Y	$783.53	$1,283.53
ED STUDIES	E	$40	1437	292	Y	$755.58	$1,255.58
ELEMENTARY	E	$40	1823	1093	Y	$1,268.30	$1,768.30
ENGLISH	L	$45	2651	153	Y	$931.11	$1,431.11
FOREIGN LANG	L	$45	376	17	-	$320.82	$820.82
GERONTOLOGY	E	$40	154	42	-	$266.55	$766.55
HEALTH AND PHYS ED	E	$40	768	0	-	$357.33	$857.33
HISTORY	L	$45	722	90	-	$425.22	$925.22
INDUSTRY & TECH	S	$62	1114	520	Y	$939.38	$1,439.38
MATH/COMP	S	$62	3003	280	Y	$1,157.67	$1,657.67
MUSIC	L	$45	461	0	-	$327.23	$827.23
NURSING	S	$62	146	191	-	$465.29	$965.29
PHILOSOPHY	L	$45	499	8	-	$338.69	$838.69
PHYSICAL SCI	S	$62	1401	84	-	$639.19	$1,139.19
PSYCHOLOGY	L	$45	1555	285	Y	$800.47	$1,300.47
SOCIAL SCI	L	$45	1637	251	Y	$796.96	$1,296.96
SOCIAL WORK	E	$40	537	132	-	$387.17	$887.17
SPECIAL ED	E	$40	1020	117	Y	$581.85	$1,081.85
SPEECH PATH & AUD	E	$40	235	190	Y	$476.41	$976.41
SPORTS MEDICINE	S	$62	433	127	Y	$596.62	$1,096.62
THEATER	L	$45	278	19	-	$303.74	$803.74
TOTALS		$1,266	27,490	6,174		$17,000	$30,000

WEIGHTS DESIRED (ALL THREE MUST SUM TO 100):

BOOK COST	40
NO. ENROLLEES	30
NO. MAJORS	20
GRAD PROGRAM	10
TOT AVAIL $	17,000
ADJUSTED AMOUNT $	500
	13000

COST PER AVERAGE BOOK IN EACH FIELD:

EDUCATION	$40
LIBERAL ARTS	$45
SCIENCE / TECH	$62

CATAWBA MODIFIED CLAPP-JORDAN FORMULA
FOR THE LIBRARY ACCESS BUDGET

The following describes the background of the formula figures and the factors used.

The formula derives from research carried out by Verner W. Clapp and Robert T. Jordan in the 1950's and 1960's on how libraries grow and what quantitative criteria could be identified to assist in planning for library budgets. What factors in each institution could be identified and used to reflect that institutions' needs and programs. Clapp and Jordan attempted to develop a "formula" which would take into account "the principal factors that affect the requirements for [materials] in connection with academic programs and in which each factor would be weighed in a manner capable of being related to and justified by practice".[1]

PLEASE NOTE: This formula is aimed at determining minimum adequacy of growth. Given the Catawba budget in past years, it is evident that we do not even achieve minimum -- in fact, we have received less than one third of the minimum.

I have assumed that the Catawba Library collections will double every ten years. Since we are not a research library, this does not mean that the physical space of the library grows by double, but that we will weed out-of-date materials as new ones come in. This assumption of doubling every ten years is based on the rapid pace of publishing and growth of knowledge. In the sciences, for instance, the shelf life of a book is less than five (5) years. (By shelf life, I mean that the information contained in them is still valid.) In the social sciences, it is about the same. The humanities materials have a somewhat longer shelf life of ten to fifteen years. Business materials have a shelf life of about five to ten years.

In some areas, such as the sciences, it may be wise for us to consider not purchasing books and some expensive periodicals which may be lightly used. Instead we may want to use that money to buy online access to journal databases from which we would provide hard copy printouts or floppy disc copies for which we would charge the patron nothing. In the long run it will be cheaper to do this than to acquire, catalog and house these materials. This is an area which we will need to monitor closely as the rapid expansion of electronic publishing continues.

[1]Clapp, Verner W. and Robert W. Jordan. "Quantitative Criteria for Adequacy of Academic Library Collections", College and Research Libraries, p. 371-380. September, 1965.

The Catawba modified Clapp-Jordan formula has the following factors for the relationship of books and periodicals to the student body, the faculty and the curriculum for estimating the size for minimal adequacy growth.

For each of the above use the following:

	BOOKS		PERIODICALS	
Faculty	6/year x 10 =	60	1.5/year x 10 =	15
Students	1/year x 10 =	10	.1/year x 10 =	10
Undergraduate programs	24/year x 10 =	240*	.3/year x 10 =	3*
Masters degree programs	240/year x 10 =	2,400*	1/year x 10 =	10*

*These figures are represented in the formula as each department's share of the basic collection.

Catawba College

FORMULA FACTORS

1. The student body: size and composition--
                          Undergraduate/Graduate

2. The faculty: size

3. The curriculum: number of courses

4. The cost of library
    materials: delivered to Salisbury, NC

THE STUDENT BODY

The number of FTE students is calculated by the number of credit
hours per semester for undergraduates and masters courses. We
obtain the registrar's printouts for the Fall and Spring
semesters only. These are charted by course and the number of
hours at each level and averaged.

THE FACULTY

The number of FTE faculty is calculated by the number of courses
taught per semester. We obtain the registrar's printouts for the
Fall and Spring semesters only. The number of courses at each
level of undergraduate and graduate are counted and averaged.
(This results in a different number for FTE faculty than is used
by the administration.)

THE CURRICULUM

While the basic collection was figured by majors and minors, we
found that was impossible to do on an annual basis as many
courses count toward two or three different majors or minors
within a department. For this reason, we have used the
departments to figure annual budget.

THE COST OF LIBRARY MATERIALS

For this initial figuring of the formula, I have used standard
prices for all materials. As we implement the formula, it will
be possible to figure Catawba's average costs and use those in
the formula.

THE TABLES IN THE FORMULA DOCUMENT

TABLE A: DEGREES OFFERED

This is a photocopy of the list from the current edition of the
Catawba Catalog.

TABLE B: FTE CREDIT HOURS BY DEPARTMENT

This table shows the average number of FTE credit hours by department. The procedure for calculating is as follows:

1. Compute the average of the Fall and Spring semester undergraduate and graduate credit hours.

2. Divide the average of the undergraduate hours by 15 to get the FTECH.

3. Divide the average of the graduate hours by 12 to get the FTECH.

TABLE C: FULL-TIME FACULTY BY DEPARTMENT

This table shows the average number of FTE faculty by department. The procedure for calculating is as follows:

1. Compute the average number of the Fall and Spring semester undergraduate and graduate courses offered.

2. Divide the average number of courses offered by 4 to get the FTEF.

TABLE D: DEPARTMENTAL ALLOCATIONS

This table shows the annual minimal budget for each department. The procedure for calculations is as follows:

1. Multiply the FTEF times the number of books to be acquired per year (6).

2. Multiply the FTEF times the number of periodicals to be acquired per year (1.5).

3. Multiply the FTECH times the number of book to be acquired per year (1).

4. Multiply the FTECH times the number of periodicals to be acquired per year (.1).

5. Multiply the departmental percentage of the total number of FTECH times the number of periodicals in the basic collection (565) to obtain each department's share of periodical titles in the basic collection.

TABLE E: DIVISIONAL ALLOCATIONS

This table summarizes each department's allocation by division.

TABLE F: MINIMUM MATERIALS BUDGET

This table summarizes each department's allocation.

TABLE G: BASIC COLLECTION

This table summarizes, by department, the size of the basic collection. I have pro rated the serials to each department in Table D, but not the books. The serials are an ongoing expense so have to be accounted for each year. The books are a one time purchase and as such are already in the collection.

Columbia Union College
Theofield G. Weis Library
Takoma Park, Maryland

Basis for Materials Budget Allocation

The library's materials budget is divided into non-departmental and departmental segments. The non-departmental segment is comprised of such categories as general and cultural works, indexes, library science professional materials, lost-book replacement, reference works, periodicals, and electronic databases. The library director sets aside a projected amount for each of the above categories. The balance of the library's funds for materials is allocated to individual academic departments rather than treated as an undivided whole. The allocation is made on the basis of the courses each department offers as listed in the current college catalog. The formula used is adapted from one believed to have once been used at the University of Southern California.

The course offerings are scored on the basis of the number of semester hours listed in the catalog for each course:

(a) The number of semester hours times 2 (Upper Division)
(b) The number of semester hours times 1 (Lower Division)

One-half point is counted for each semester hour in observation teaching and lower division mathematics.

Zero is counted for all courses based mainly on performance skills, such as keyboarding; vocal and instrumental music lessons (individual and group); elementary, intermediate, and conversational language courses; and practicums.

Courses which earn no credit are also counted as zero.

The following formula is used: $(a \times 2)$; $(b \times 1)$; $\dfrac{(b \times 1)}{2}$

Courses that are cross-listed in more than one department are counted in the department in which they are taught.

The total points for each department are added to reach a grand total for the catalog. The departmental book funds available for a given year are divided by the grand total to give a dollar amount per point. Then, the individual department total points are multiplied by the dollar figure to reach the allocation per department.

One factor that is not taken into account in the above formula is that of supporting classes that have large enrollments which may require multiple copies of some materials. This need is met on an individual basis as the situation warrants. A second such factor involves the high cost of books in some disciplines. This problem is also handled as it arises. Generally speaking, the library orders most of the materials which a department requests in a given year.

Library of Davidson College
Davidson College
Davidson, NC

We have one budget.....a materials budget (it is 'fed' by two financial line items but that is based on the source of the funds-- endowed or general-- not based on use). 40% of the budget is traditionally under the control of the library; 60% is given to the library committee to divide up.

First from that 60% we take the small funding that we give to a few programs and concentrations.....e.g. ROTC, PE, Center for Special Studies, South Asian Studies, and the like.

The balance goes to the departments

The division based on 5 factors.....each equally weighted:

* number of SENIOR majors in a department
* number of FTE faculty members in a department
* number of students taught by that department based on its purchases through our library, not the published rates.
* average periodical/serial price for that department based on its purchases through our library, not the published rates

For each of these categories, each is made a % of the total. E.G......if the history department has 50 majors.....you add all of the department's majors, and what percentage is that of the total of all majors. And that is done for each department in each category.

Then the categories are computed horizontally.....all of the %s in each of the categories for the history department are added together.....say 5%, 10%. 3%. etc. That total for each department.....is then converted to a % of the total of all of the departments.

The resulting figure or % is then applied to the bass amount and that gives the amount they are allocated. We have it set up on a spread sheet and plug in the figures and it comes out easily.

SAMPLE DEPARTMENTAL BUDGET ALLOCATION FORMULA

In a small academic institution, careful selection of materials is especially important because of limited funds and the pressing need to have those purchases, in the main, support directly the academic offerings. The Committee feels, too, that the way this is done is the prerogative of the individual departments/programs and wished in no way to prescribe how this should be done.

However, the Committee would like to present for consideration the following method which several departments/programs have adopted and which, in the opinion of the Committee, appears to assure an orderly and even growth of the collection in the various disciplines:

A. All periodicals/standing orders which at least two members of a department/program consider necessary for their courses should be paid "off the top" of the departmental/program's allotment;

B. Next, the funds remaining are divided equally among the members of the department/program. From this the professor may order periodicals and books.

C. Among the members of the department/program, areas of concern, specialities, and specific courses are identified for which the individual professors are charged with buying library materials.

This procedure seems to be equitable in that it allows each department to take those periodicals, etc., which are considered important for a sound program. Also, it assured that the funds spent relatively evenly building up the collection in the Library viz-a-viz the academic offerings at Davidson.

Frederick W. Crumb Memorial Library
SUNY at Potsdam
Potsdam, New York

PROPOSED FORMULA
for allocating
Departmental S/O & Monographic Budgets

FACTORS:

Credits:

Credit hours were calculated using the average number of credit hours taught in each department over the four most recent semesters.
The number of credit hours was multiplied by the following weighting factors:

Lower undergraduate hours	1
Upper undergraduate hours	2.5
Graduate hours	1.25

Students:

Student FTE were averaged over the most recent four semesters based on Potsdam College Department Profiles.

Materials costs:

The average cost of a book in the discipline was based on tables published in CHOICE (March 1993).

Number of titles:

The number of titles published in each discipline was based on the number of titles reviewed in CHOICE in 1992 (March 1993).

Use:

At present, not included. We have no use statistics available.

FORMULA:

Using terms defined above:

Credits X Students X Cost X Number of titles

GIVEN:

Each department was allocated at least as much this year as was allocated last year in the combined S/O -monographic budget. The inflationary increase of $6445 was allocated to departments that are underfunded according to this formula.

Periodical costs are not included.